21st CENTURY SKILLS LIBRARY

INSIDE U.S. ELECTIONS

POLITICAL PARTIES

by Samantha Bell

CHERRY LAKE PRESS

Published in the United States of America by
Cherry Lake Publishing Group
Ann Arbor, Michigan
www.cherrylakepublishing.com

Reading Adviser: Beth Walker Gambro, MS, Ed., Reading Consultant, Yorkville, IL

Content Editor: Mark Richards, Ph.D., Professor, Dept. of Political Science, Grand Valley State University, Allendale, MI

Photo Credits: © PeskyMonkey/iStock.com, cover, title page; © ungvar/Shutterstock, 5; © chrisdorney/Shutterstock, 6; Records of the National Woman's Party, Prints and Photographs Division, Library of Congress, 8; Fibonacci Blue from Minnesota, USA, CC BY 2.0 via Wikimedia Commons, 10; © MMD Creative/Shutterstock, 11; © Rachael Warriner/Shutterstock, 13; The White House from Washington, DC, Public domain, via Wikimedia Commons, 14; Gage Skidmore from Peoria, AZ, United States of America, CC BY-SA 2.0 via Wikimedia Commons, 15; United States Federal Government, Public domain, via Wikimedia Commons, 17; Gage Skidmore from Peoria, AZ, United States of America, CC BY-SA 2.0 via Wikimedia Commons, 18; © Andrew Cline/Shutterstock, 21; © Rob Crandall/Shutterstock, 22; © Studio Romantic/Shutterstock, 23; © Rawpixel.com/Shutterstock, 25; © Luoxi/Shutterstock, 26; © gpointstudio/Shutterstock, 29; © Ground Picture/Shutterstock, 31; © txking/Shutterstock, 32; © Rawpixel.com/Shutterstock, 33; Molly Theobald, for the aflcio2008, CC BY 2.0 via Wikimedia Commons, 34; © James Andrews1/Shutterstock, 37; Gage Skidmore from Surprise, AZ, United States of America, CC BY-SA 2.0 via Wikimedia Commons, 38; Gage Skidmore from Surprise, AZ, United States of America, CC BY-SA 2.0 via Wikimedia Commons, 40; © Black Salmon/Shutterstock, 41; The White House from Washington, DC, Public domain, via Wikimedia Commons, 42

Copyright © 2025 by Cherry Lake Publishing

All rights reserved. No part of this book may be reproduced or utilized in any form or by any means without written permission from the publisher.

Cherry Lake Press is an imprint of Cherry Lake Publishing Group.

Library of Congress Cataloging-in-Publication Data has been filed and is available at catalog.loc.gov

Printed in the United States of America

Note from Publisher: Websites change regularly, and their future contents are outside of our control. Supervise children when conducting any recommended online searches for extended learning opportunities.

CONTENTS

CHAPTER 1   4
Types of Parties

CHAPTER 2   12
Platforms and Planks

CHAPTER 3   20
Choosing a Party—Or Not

CHAPTER 4   28
Gathering Support

CHAPTER 5   36
Raising Funds

Activity   44
Glossary   46
To Learn More   47
Index   48
About the Author   48

CHAPTER 1

TYPES OF PARTIES

A political party is a group of people that have similar political ideas. The members of the party support many of the same **policies**. The main goal of a political party is to get its members into government positions. That way, the party can work to carry out these policies.

Government has several levels. Each level has different positions. Some are at the local level. These include city or county offices such as the mayor and council members. Other positions are at the state level. These include the governor and state legislators. There are also positions at the national level. These include senators, representatives, and the president.

The U.S. began operating under the Constitution on March 9, 1789.

In the United States, all of these government officials are chosen through elections. Part of this process is described in the Constitution. This document explains the powers of the government. It also states the rights of the people. But the Constitution does not mention political parties. Many of the **Founding Fathers** did not trust political parties. They thought that political parties could become too powerful.

George Washington was the first president of the United States. He became president in 1789. He served two terms. Early in his first term, two new political parties formed. Since then, there have been

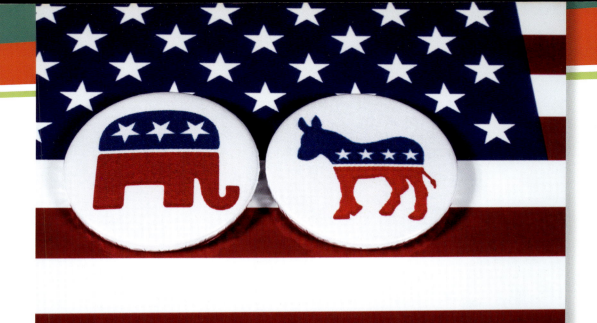

The symbol for Democrats in the United States is a donkey. The symbol for Republicans is an elephant.

two major parties during most of U.S. history. Today, these parties are the Democrats and the Republicans. The Republicans are sometimes called the GOP. This stands for Grand Old Party.

Democrats and Republicans hold different positions on many **issues**. For example, many Democrats believe the national government should do more to take care of its citizens. They approve when the government gets involved in businesses and industries.

Republicans tend to have a different view. Many think the government should play a smaller role in people's lives. They believe the government should make it easier for people to do things for themselves.

Both parties have logos to represent them. The Democrats' unofficial logo is a donkey. The Republicans' logo is an elephant. These were made popular by a cartoonist in the 1800s. They are still used today.

THIRD PARTIES

Democrats and Republicans are the two main political parties in the United States. But they aren't the only ones. Smaller parties are known as third parties. People who aren't satisfied with the two big parties may join a third party.

Third parties usually focus on certain issues. For example, the Green Party is a third party. It focuses on the environment. The Libertarian Party is another third party. One of its goals is to reduce the power of the national government.

Some third parties don't last. This can happen if they were formed to promote a certain issue. In 1872, the Equal Rights Party demanded that women have a right

These American women marched for women's right to vote in 1914. Though the Equal Rights Party officially disbanded in 1888, women didn't win the right to vote until 1920.

to vote. Women won that right in 1920. The party no longer exists.

Some third parties grow around certain leaders. In 1992, businessman Ross Perot created the Reform Party. He didn't win the election. The party has not had another **candidate** in many years. Over the years, many third parties have come and gone.

THE IMPORTANCE OF THIRD PARTIES

Third-party candidates have never been elected President. But they are still important in national elections. They give supporters a way to voice their opinions on the issues. For example, someone may disagree with the two main parties on a certain issue. The third party provides them with a way to express it.

Third-party candidates also help make people aware of certain issues. They may gain a lot of support. This can raise an issue to the national level. Then one of the two main parties may support the issue too.

Third-party candidates can influence elections in another way. Sometimes an election is close.

The Libertarian Party is a third party in U.S. politics.

No party has a big lead in votes. When this happens, third parties can impact who the winner will be. When people vote for a third party, they don't vote for the Democrats or Republicans. Either the Democrats or Republicans will lose votes they would have had otherwise. Then the other major party will likely win.

The two-party system isn't perfect. But the United States has used it for more than 200 years. After each election, Americans hope their party will do a good job representing them.

FUN FACT: THE PIZZA PARTY

In 2014, a man from Boston, Massachusetts, founded the Pizza Party. The party has more than 180 members. It has enough members to run for a state office. But the party is not an official political party. The party supports cheese pizza. They also support adding toppings.

CHAPTER 2
PLATFORMS AND PLANKS

Every 4 years, the Democrats and Republicans each choose a candidate to run for president. Before the election, each party creates a new party platform. The party platform is a written document. It states the goals and **principles** the party stands for. It also states the party's position on important issues.

The party platform is made up of planks. A plank is a position the party takes on a certain issue. For example, one of the issues might be climate change. The plank shares the party's view on climate change and how it would address the issue. Other issues that parties take positions on include health care and the economy. These positions would be other planks in their platform.

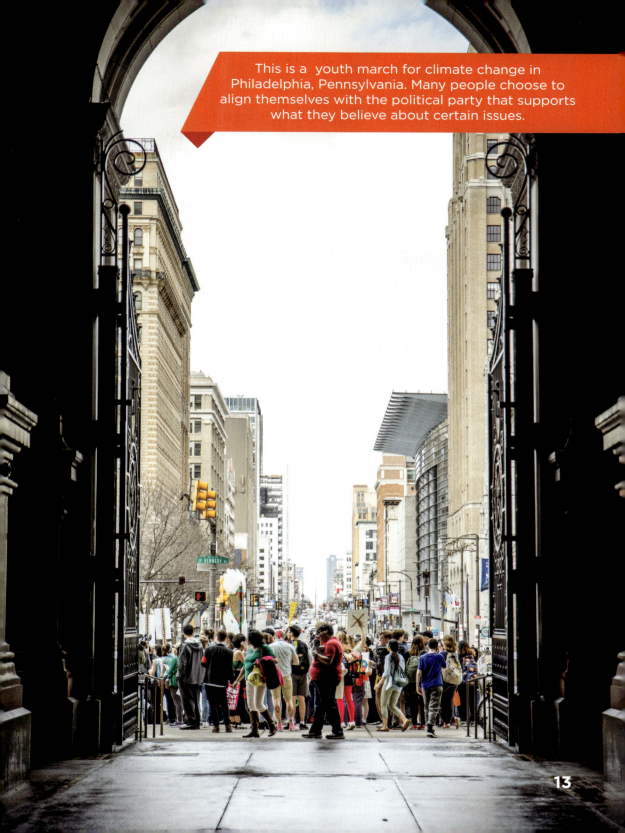

This is a youth march for climate change in Philadelphia, Pennsylvania. Many people choose to align themselves with the political party that supports what they believe about certain issues.

Barack Obama greeting Democratic National Committee members.

CREATING A PLATFORM

When a party's candidate is running against a current president, the party needs to create a new platform. Creating a platform begins with the platform committee. The party selects the people who will be on the committee. This includes well-known party members. The members represent different states. They also represent different **interest groups**.

The committee starts by holding **hearings**. Some of these are in person. They can take place all around the country. Other hearings are online.

Ronna McDaniel was the longest serving female chair of either major U.S. party. She was the chair of the Republican National Committee.

The committee wants to know what other party members think about the issues.

The committee talks about the platform. They have debates about the positions the party should take. Then they vote on those positions. When the positions are approved, they become planks. A platform often has many planks. The platform can cover many issues.

The platform isn't final yet. It still must be approved by the party. The party holds a **national convention**. The committee brings the platform to the convention. Party members consider the platform. Some issues may be debated again. Finally, the platform is officially adopted.

The platform expresses the party's view on current issues. Sometimes the issues change. The party's position may change too. When this happens, the party will write a new platform before the next election.

The new platform will follow the same process. The committee will hold hearings. They will debate the positions. Then they'll write the new

Donald Trump controlled the Republican platform when he ran as incumbent for president in 2020.

platform. It will then go to the national convention to be approved again.

Sometimes the party's candidate is already the president. Presidents finishing their first term usually run for a second term. When this happens, the president controls the platform. They want to make sure they agree with all the planks.

IMPORTANCE OF PLATFORMS

Some people think party platforms don't really matter. Many people never read their party's platform.

Sometimes the candidates don't even read it. Also, candidates don't have to follow their party's platform. They can choose to take different positions on the issues.

But platforms are still important to the election process. Platforms give people a clear idea of the party's position on the issues. Some candidates use

Dr. Jill Stein is part of the U.S. Green Party. Ecological wisdom and sustainability are two of their key values. These key values are part of their platform.

this information in their campaigns. That way, voters better understand what the candidates stand for. People can make a good guess about how a candidate will behave in office. Most presidents make an effort to follow the party platform.

PERSPECTIVES: ACCOUNTABILITY

Candidates say they will do many things if they are elected. These are called campaign promises. They make these promises so people will vote for them. For example, one of the most common promises is reducing taxes. Another is increasing the number of jobs available. A candidate can get more votes if people believe their promises.

But campaign promises are often hard to keep. The elected candidate may try. But they may not have enough support from Congress. If the candidate runs again, the voters usually remember the broken promises. They may feel like the candidate lied. They may not vote for them a second time.

CHAPTER 3
CHOOSING A PARTY—OR NOT

People can join a political party when they sign up to vote. It is not required. There is no cost to join. They just choose the party that shares their values and beliefs. People can change their political party at any time.

People may not agree with every part of their party's platform. But they usually agree with the issues that are most important to them. For example, someone may strongly believe that health care should be free. They then can choose the party that most closely agrees with them. People can find out any party's position by reading its platform.

The biggest benefit to choosing a party is being able to vote in a primary election. Primary elections are also called primaries. Each political party holds their own primaries. All of the candidates are members of that party.

Republican Nikki Haley spoke at a rally during the 2024 New Hampshire Republican primary. She won 43.2 percent of the votes. Donald Trump won 54.3 percent of the votes.

By voting in the primary, party members decide their candidate in the general election. The newly chosen Republican candidate will run against the newly chosen Democratic candidate. Third-party candidates will run in this election too. In a general election, people can vote for any of the candidates. They don't have to vote for their party's candidate.

VOTING INDEPENDENT

People don't have to join a political party in order to vote. When they register to vote, they can mark that they don't want to join a party at all.

Voters don't have to choose a political party in order to vote.

People who don't join a party are known as independents.

Some independents agree more with the Democratic Party. Some agree more with the Republican Party. Some don't agree with either party. Younger people who are independents are often in this last group. They may vote for a third party. Some don't vote at all.

23

Many independents have negative views about political parties. They think that government leaders should work together. They don't like it when leaders fight and argue. Some independents don't think that electing a new leader will improve things. They don't think politicians keep their promises.

Independents often feel discouraged. They want more options than the two main parties give them. Some states don't let independents vote in primaries. It seems like their votes aren't as important. They may feel like they are ignored.

INDEPENDENTS MATTER

Independents are sometimes called "swing voters." This is because the number of Republican and Democratic votes is often close. Votes from independents can "swing" the election in favor of one or the other party. Their votes often help determine major elections.

Sometimes, independent voters feel like their votes don't matter. However, these independent votes can decide the winner!

Many different factors influence someone's political beliefs. Many young people are passionate about environmental issues.

The two big political parties try to win the votes of the independents. But this isn't easy. Independents often hold different views than the party. They may even hold different views from each other. The two biggest political parties must convince independents that they are the best choice.

SPOTLIGHT ON: FAMILY INFLUENCE

A young person's political views are often shaped by many things. These can include their friends, their teachers, and even the media. Their families are also a big influence. According to a recent survey, most teens join the same political party as their parents.

Many parents discuss politics with their teens. It is a good way for teens to learn about different political views. During an election, parents and kids can talk about who is running for office. They can discuss the party platforms. Parents can tell their teens who they are voting for and why. This is one way teens learn how to make political decisions.

CHAPTER 4
GATHERING SUPPORT

Voters are citizens who have registered to vote. Voting is a way they can show where they stand on the issues. It's a way to make their voices heard. But in every election, there are many voters who don't vote.

Voters have different reasons for not voting. Sometimes they may not like any of the candidates who are running. They may feel like the candidates don't support their views. They may disagree with the party platforms.

Some voters don't vote because they are discouraged. They don't think the political system works very well. They may want things to be different. But they don't believe new leaders in government will change things. They think their vote doesn't matter.

Political parties know that every vote counts. That is why they try to **motivate** their party members to vote.

Some voters struggle with feeling like their vote doesn't matter. They get discouraged by the state of the world and the decisions politicians make.

They also try to encourage independents to vote for them. With enough votes, they can win the elections.

REACHING THE VOTERS

Political parties use different strategies to encourage people to vote. One of these is canvassing. Party members go from house to house. They knock on the doors and try to talk to the residents. They share information about the candidates. They encourage people to vote. They remind the voters about the election date so they won't miss it.

Phone banking is another way that parties encourage voters. Phone banking is when party members make calls to voters. They may ask them to vote for a certain candidate. They might help voters learn how to get to the **polls**.

Party members may also talk to voters about their voting plans. They can help voters decide when they will go to the polling place. They also help them figure out how they will get there. Having a plan increases the chance that they will actually vote.

Political parties sometimes send out texts to party members who have agreed to receive them. This is only one way they try to reach voters.

Texting is another way parties reach out to voters. Texting allows parties to share a message with hundreds of people at once. Sometimes a voter responds. Then a party member can have a conversation with them. They can answer the voter's questions. They can send the voter information about their polling place. They can help them make a plan to vote. Texting is especially helpful for connecting with younger voters.

Political parties also use social media platforms to encourage voters. Social media helps them reach a lot

Social media is a tool many politicians and campaigns use to encourage people to vote.

of people quickly. Parties might use social media to explain how to register to vote. They may tell people how to check to make sure they are registered. They can stress the importance of voting.

These types of social media posts have pushed younger voters to get involved. Many young people get their political news from social media. They use the platforms to share their opinions about the issues. Parties can connect with them online. They can show them the importance of voting.

Another way to reach voters is by holding political events. These can include rallies. A rally is a large gathering of people. The party leaders or candidates give speeches. They discuss their platforms and try to get more support. Another type of event is a town hall meeting. At a town hall meeting, voters can ask the candidates questions. The candidates answer the voters directly.

VOLUNTEERS

All of these strategies take a lot of time and work. The candidates and their teams can't do it by themselves. They depend on other party members to help. These

Volunteers are often people who are passionate about a particular political candidate or that candidate's platform.

members volunteer their time. They don't get paid for their work. They just want to help their candidate win.

Volunteers fill many roles. They register people to vote. They go canvassing door-to-door. They represent the candidate in a friendly way. They share the candidate's message directly with the community. They make phone calls and send texts. They inform and persuade voters. During events, volunteers make sure everything runs smoothly.

People younger than 18 usually cannot vote. But they can volunteer. Parties with teen volunteers are often able to reach more voters. They especially reach more young voters. These voters may be more likely to listen to someone close to their age.

Volunteering has another benefit for teens. They learn political and communication skills. They also learn that their political opinions and actions matter.

TRUE STORY: REACHING THE YOUTH

In the 1992 presidential election, Bill Clinton ran against President George H. W. Bush. During the campaign, Bush seemed to ignore young voters. But Clinton reached out to them. He visited college campuses and gave speeches. Thousands of students registered to vote. Others joined his campaign as volunteers.

Clinton also connected with young people through the media. He went on MTV to answer their questions. He played the saxophone on a late-night show. His actions led to a huge increase in the number of young people voting. Close to half of voters aged 18 to 24 voted for Clinton. He won the presidency.

CHAPTER 5

RAISING FUNDS

Political campaigns take a lot of work. The campaign staff, party members, and volunteers all put in a huge effort. They want to help their candidates win. But campaigns take more than just hard work. They also require a lot of money.

Campaigns have many expenses. These include printed materials. Campaigns use **brochures** and flyers to tell voters about their candidates. These are often one-page documents that describe the candidate's platform. They may also include the candidate's **biography**. Other printed material includes posters and banners with the candidate's picture and campaign message. These may be displayed on street corners or at events.

Most campaigns have a headquarters. This is a building or offices used to run the campaign. The

Joe Biden's 2020 campaign cost over $1,000,000. Almost 80 percent of that money went to fund media, including printed materials like signs, brochures, and flyers.

campaign often rents this space until the election is over. The campaign staff works at the headquarters. The staff are paid for the work they do. At the headquarters, staff members use equipment such as computers and printers. They need office supplies like paper and tape. All of these supplies cost money.

Campaigns have many other expenses. Ads on television, the radio, and the internet are expensive. Expenses also include food and supplies for rallies, meetings, and other campaign activities. Money is also used for items to promote the candidate. These include things such as T-shirts, stickers, and yard signs. The cost of these smaller items quickly adds up.

FINDING DONATIONS

The candidates can't pay for all of these things themselves. Sometimes the party provides some money. But candidates still have to raise more. This is known as fundraising.

Fundraising takes a lot of time. A candidate must constantly look for people and businesses to support them financially. The money they give is called a donation. Candidates need many donations to keep their campaigns going.

Some donations come from political action committees, or PACs. These committees are created by corporations and other organizations. Corporations are not allowed to donate to campaigns. But they can give money to the PAC. The PAC can then give it to the campaign.

Some donations are given by individuals. These are divided into two groups. Large donations are more than $200. Small donations are less than $200. Candidates can also donate money to their own campaigns. All of these donations add up. In presidential elections, it can equal billions of dollars.

Candidates request donations in different ways. They can use websites to collect money online. They can send emails or letters to party members. Campaign volunteers may also make phone calls asking for donations.

Laws limit how much people can donate to a campaign. This is to make sure the election is fair. Someone who gives a very large amount may have too much influence over the candidate.

Sometimes, volunteers gather together to all make calls for a certain campaign. They may call people to ask for donations.

Many people donate to their preferred political candidate's campaign online.

RAISING FUNDS

Besides collecting donations, candidates can also raise money for their campaigns. One way they do this is by holding special events. These events usually require tickets. The money from the tickets is donated to the campaign.

Events may be any size. For example, the campaign could host a huge party with special guests. Or it could hold a simple event in a park or backyard.

Many events were held virtually during the COVID-19 pandemic. Donald Trump held a virtual town hall with Fox News at the Lincoln Memorial.

Almost any type of in-person event can be a campaign fundraiser.

Fundraising events can also be online. Virtual events can help candidates connect with supporters wherever they are. They usually require less planning than in-person events.

Political parties play an important role in elections. They tell voters what the candidates stand for. They allow people to express different views. They unite voters who believe in the same things. They provide ways for citizens of all ages to get involved in government.

PERSPECTIVES: THE IMPORTANCE OF SMALL DONATIONS

Many large donations come from wealthy individuals. Some come from special interest groups. It may seem like these are the most important donations. They provide huge amounts of money for the candidates. But small donations are better for both the candidates and the voters.

It takes many small donations to equal one large one. But this means that many people donated money. The money represents more of the voters. More people are supporting the candidate. This makes the relationship between the candidate and the voters stronger. The candidate can better represent their community.

ACTIVITY

CREATE YOUR OWN PARTY PLATFORM

A party platform defines a party's goals and values. It helps to give the party a common purpose. It also helps to keep the party focused on key issues. If you started your own political party, what would your platform be? What ideas would other people help you work on?

Create your own party platform based around issues important in your life.

1. **Make a list of at least five issues at your school or neighborhood.**

Start by thinking of some things that could be issues at your school or neighborhood. Some issues at your school can include the amount of homework or the cost of field trips. Issues in your neighborhood might include the size of the sidewalks or dogs on leashes.

2. **Choose a position on each issue you listed.**

Look at the issues you picked. Think about where you stand with each one. For example, do you think students have too much homework? Or maybe you think they don't get enough. Do you think families should pay for field trips? Or should they be free? Are the sidewalks in your neighborhood the right size? Is there enough room to ride a bike? Should people keep their dogs on leashes? Or do dogs need room to run? Maybe the neighborhood needs a dog park.

3. Write your position beside each issue.
Include plenty of detail. Explain what you think should happen. These are the planks in your platform!

4. Research solutions.
A party platform can be more than just goals for what should be. It should include a path towards accomplishing those goals. Research each issue by reading up on it, talking to school or local officials, and talking to your friends and family to find out what they think. Write down steps for how people can work together to make the goal happen. For example, cutting down homework by making sure students can show their knowledge in other ways during class time.

5. Develop your pitch.
A party isn't a party without more people. How will you convince others to join your party? Why are your ideas and solutions the way to go? Create slogans to catch people's attention and make your ideas memorable. Find ways to talk about the problem with leaving things as they are.

Now, go out and make a difference with supporters by your side. Welcome to politics!

GLOSSARY

biography (bye-AH-gruh-fee) a written story of the facts and events of a person's life

brochures (broh-SHURZ) small booklets that contain pictures and is used for advertising

candidate (KAN-duh-dayt) a person who wants to be elected to a certain position

Founding Fathers (FOWN-ding FAA-thuhrz) leaders who started the United States that included members of the convention that wrote the U.S. Constitution

hearings (HEER-ingz) meetings to get information and opinions

interest groups (IN-truhst GROOPS) people with a common concern who work together

issues (IH-shooz) important subjects or concerns

motivate (MOH-tuh-vayt) to inspire someone to do something

national convention (NA-shuh-nuhl kuhn-VEN-shun) a meeting of members of a political party at the national level to decide which candidates will run for office

policies (PAH-luh-seez) rules or guidelines that people follow

polls (POHLZ) places where people go to vote in an election

principles (PRIN-suh-puhlz) a set of rules a person follows

TO LEARN MORE

BOOKS

Berne, Emma Carlson, Cari Meister, and Nel Yomtov. *The Kids' Complete Guide to Elections.* North Mankato, MN: Capstone Press, 2020.

Meister, Cari. *Political Parties: A Kid's Guide*. North Mankato, MN: Capstone Press, 2020.

Weber, M. *Political Parties*. Mankato, MN: Child's World, Inc., 2020.

WEBSITES

Search these online sources with an adult:

"Political Parties." Scholastic.

"Political Parties – U.S. Government for Kids!" Miacademy Learning Channel.

"Should We Have More Than 2 Major Political Parties?" PBS Learning.

INDEX

Biden, Joe, 37, 38, 40
Bush, George H. W., 35

campaign fundraising, 36–43
campaign promises, 18, 24
canvassing, 30, 34
Clinton, Bill, 35
communication with voters, 30–35, 36, 38

Democratic National Committee, 14
Democratic Party, 6

elections
    government systems, 5, 12, 20–22, 24
    party alignment, 22–23
    primaries, 20–21, 24
    third party effects, 9–10
Equal Rights Party, 7–9

Green Party, 7, 18

Haley, Nikki, 21

independent/swing voters, 22–25, 27
issues and policies
    party support and goals, 4, 6–9, 12–13, 16, 18–19, 20, 43
    personal beliefs, 20, 23–24, 26, 27, 28, 44
    platforms and planks, 12–19, 44–45

Libertarian Party, 7, 10

McDaniel, Ronna, 15

phone and text banking, 30–31, 34, 40
platforms and planks, 12–19, 44–45
political parties, 4
    alignment and voting, 20–27, 28
    history, 5–10
political protest, 8, 10, 13, 26
presidential elections, 5, 12, 17, 35, 37, 39–40

Reform Party, 9
Republican National Committee, 15
Republican Party, 6–7, 21

social media, 31–32
Stein, Jill, 18

third parties, 7–10, 23
Trump, Donald, 17, 32, 42
two-party systems, 5–7, 9–10, 23–25, 27

volunteers, 33–35, 36, 38, 40
voting
    participation choices, 23–24, 28–30
    party encouragement, 28, 30–35
    processes, 22–23, 30, 32
    women's rights, 7–9

Washington, George, 5

youth vote, 23, 27, 31, 32, 34–35

ABOUT THE AUTHOR

Samantha Bell was born and raised near Orlando, Florida. She grew up in a family of eight kids and all kinds of pets, including goats, chickens, cats, dogs, rabbits, horses, parakeets, hamsters, guinea pigs, a monkey, a raccoon, and a coatimundi. She now lives with her family in the foothills of the Blue Ridge Mountains, where she enjoys hiking, painting, and snuggling with their cats, Pocket, Pebble, and Mr. Tree-Tree Triggers.